# When you are ready, where could you go?

Ron McAdow

Great Meadows Books
Lincoln, Massachusetts

Copyright 2016 Ron McAdow

ISBN: 978-0-9906084-7-9
Library of Congress Control Number: 2016957660

Great Meadows Books
59 South Great Road
Lincoln, Massachusetts 01773

*To Tony King*

*mentor and friend*

When you are ready,
where could you go?

Will you visit a farm?

You could say hello to a horse.

You might see a huge field of sunflowers.

Or wheat.

You could hike into a forest.

Will you touch the trees?
How does the bark feel under your fingers?

If you meet a fox, it will be frightened.
Not because you are mean.
Just because you are a human being.

Animals don't know how gentle you can be.

If the chipmunk becomes afraid,
it will hide among the rocks.

Plants reach out for light.

In the forest, look down for mushrooms—

—and up for birds.

Some trees grow best where the climate is cool and wet.

This tree can live where it's hot and dry.
It's a baobab.
The picture was taken in Africa.

If you go to Africa, watch for large animals.
This one is a buffalo.

You might see a zebra!

And elephants!

Is this one annoyed?

Sometimes elephants look sleepy.

Isn't it nice to feel good in the morning?

When you travel you will see faces
quite different from yours.

What a wonderful world you live in.
Giraffes live in it, too!

Do you like funny-looking animals?

Here's a strange creature with an odd name.
You know it. Hippopotamus.
The birds are called oxpeckers.

Many animals like the edge of the water.

Imagine having golden eyes!

Can you believe it?
The manatee is beside a boat dock.
It wants someone to squirt it with a hose!

The heron keeps an eye on the manatee.

Most seals live where the ocean is cold.

They like to sunbathe.

Another place you could go is the American West.
Maybe you have been there.
Maybe that's where you live?

In the West you might see a coyote.

Or a pronghorn.

Or even a bison!

Does the raven feel the sun on its feathers?

When it flies along the wall of a canyon,
the raven's shadow seems to glide beside it.

No matter where you go

parents take care of their young.

It's nice to travel with a friend.
Especially when it starts to get dark.

If you are far from your own bed,
why not sleep in a tent?

After your adventures

won't it be nice to be home again?

**About the Pictures**

All photographs were taken by Ron during trips or at home in Massachusetts.

The sunny path is in Massachusetts, U.S.

The calf is in Cornwall, U.K. The horse is in Devon, U.K.

The sunflowers and wheat are in North Dakota, U.S.

The fox is in Batxter State Park, Maine, U.S.

The fawn, chipmunk, wildflowers, mushroom, and Baltimore oriole are in Massachusetts, U.S.

The giant redwoods are in California, U.S.

The baobab and the African animals are in Zambia and Zimbabwe, on safari with Betsy, Anila, and Romesh.

The first African animal shown is an African buffalo.

The tricolored heron is on Sanibel Island, Florida, U.S.

The bullfrog is in Massachusetts, U.S.

The manatee and the black-crowned night heron are in Miami, Florida, U.S.

The gray seal and the harbor seals are in Maine, U.S., near Kennebunkport.

The western landscape is in Wind River Valley, Wyoming, U.S.

The coyote and bison are in Yellowstone National Park, Wyoming, U.S.

The ravens are in Canyon de Chelly, Arizona, U.S.

The two figures on the distant ridge are in South Dakota, U.S., in Badlands National Park. They are a daughter and a mother, Molly and Debbie.

The tent is Teddy Roosevelt National Park in North Dakota, U.S.

The bluebirds are in Lincoln, Massachusetts, U.S.

The woods road is in Maine, U.S., near Kokadjo.

The background topographical maps are from the USGS Marlborough quadrangle, 1898.

Fair Haven Hill
Lake Walden
White Pond
Nine Acre Corner
Fair Haven Pond
FITCHBURG
South
Cold Brook
Pantry Brook
Round Hill
Bridge Brook

161112

www.ingramcontent.com/pod-product-compliance
Lightning Source LLC
Chambersburg PA
CBHW061931290426
44113CB00024B/2873